Step-_by_-Step
QUICK KNITS

PENNY L. REYNOLDS

Step-by-Step
QUICK KNITS

PENNY L. REYNOLDS

GUILD OF MASTER CRAFTSMAN PUBLICATIONS

First published 2006 by
Guild of Master Craftsman Publications Ltd
166 High Street, Lewes
East Sussex, BN7 1XU

ISBN 1 86108 403 X

British Cataloguing in Publication Data

A catalogue record of this book is available from the British Library.

Managing Editor Gerrie Purcell
Production Manager Hilary MacCallum
Photography Anthony Bailey
Editor Clare Miller
Designer John Hawkins

Colour reproduction by Altaimage
Printed and bound by Hing Yip Printing Co. Ltd.

Although care has been taken to ensure that the metric measurements are true and accurate, they are only conversions from imperial; they have been rounded up or down to the nearest cm, or to the nearest convenient equivalent in cases where the imperial measurements themselves are only approximate. When following the projects, use either the imperial or the metric measurements; do not mix units.

CONTENTS

INTRODUCTION

Lauded as the new yoga, knitting has come into the forefront of our crafting lives. Its resurgence can be seen on the catwalk and on the high street. Both men and women, including stars of stage and screen, now 'admit to knit'. From the delicate 2ply labour-of-love shawls, all the way to super-chunky coats, knitting is definitely back and making a statement.

Look in your local department store or craft emporium and you should get an introduction to the vast array of glorious yarns that are available. Just a quick search on the internet will bring thousands of knitting sites offering vintage museum pieces to the ultra modern, as well as a wealth of beautiful mail order yarns.

In many cities, towns and villages a knitting group can be found and provides a great opportunity to share ideas and technical advice. For both those with years of experience and the novice alike, this is a great way of developing skills. My own local knit group meets weekly and it is a fantastic way of spending a pleasant couple of hours with a cup of tea, a biscuit and the latest ideas on knitting.

A skill that was for centuries passed down from parent to child is no longer a necessity as in days gone by, but is now a terrific pastime through which to relax and explore creativity. A busy day can be easily counterpointed by a few rows of the latest project.

There will always be a place for the 4ply baby garment, of that there is no question, and so there should be – baby knits are just about the cutest thing on the planet! However, knitting is also a craft and an art form. Quick projects that use just a couple of balls are a fantastic way to express yourself through a new craft or to return to something that you learned as a child and would like to have another go at.

This book shows you how to create something fantastic in a short length of time using exciting yarns from the high street. These projects show what can be done with just a few balls of yarn, whilst still creating something beautiful for the home or to wear. They will stir the imagination and provide the keen knitter with the skills required to begin coming up with their own novel ideas for simple 'quick knits'.

MATERIALS AND TECHNIQUES

Equipment

To begin knitting as a new craft you will need to start with some basic supplies. Not all of the following items are needed for a first project but a good supply of materials is always useful.

The first thing you will need is a good pair of knitting needles for the job. Knitting needles are sized to suit yarns from super-fine to extra chunky. If the project calls for it a needle can be found that is almost the size of a broom handle, and yes, there is a corresponding yarn out there too.

Cable needles are used when moving stitches across the piece on the same row to form cables and twists. A few of the stitches are slipped onto the cable needle and this is then left either behind or in front of the work whilst the next few stitches are worked. These 'moving' stitches can then be knitted directly from the cable needle.

Straight pins are useful for holding pieces together when stitching seams on the work. Pearl or large-headed pins are easily seen in the work and do not slip through the stitches as easily as small-headed pins.

Cable needles and straight pins

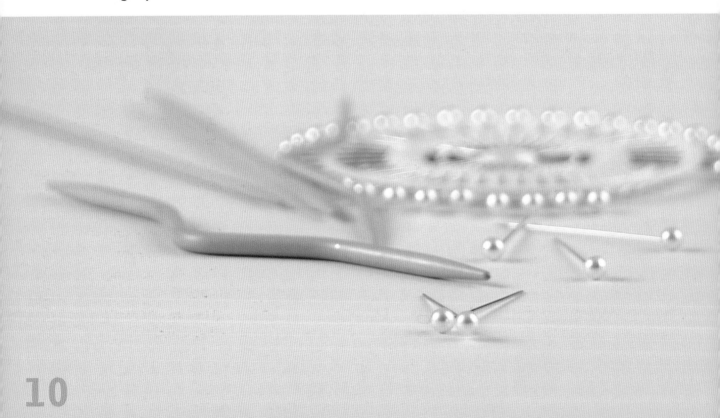

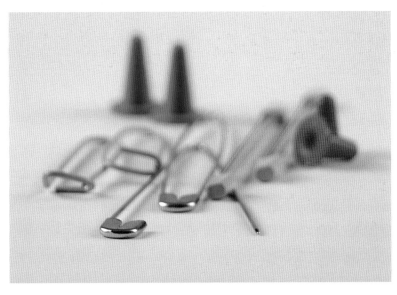

Holders can be placed on stitches not in use whilst another part of the project is completed. When these stitches are needed again there will be no seaming. Stitch holders come in several sizes to carry lots of stitches at the same time. Often when a few stitches are being held the humble nappy pin can be given a whole new lease of life as it holds a few stitches and can be locked securely whilst working on a different area.

Needle point protectors hold stitches in place on the working needles when the knitting is not being worked on.

Bobbins allow small, workable amounts of yarn to be taken from the ball when working in colours.

Crochet hooks can be used to make small running repairs; a dropped stitch can be easily picked up without the need to undo several rows of work. They are a great asset when fringing.

Large-eyed sewing needles join the pieces of work together into the finished article.

NEEDLE SIZES

Metric (mm) UK	USA	Old
2	0	14
2.25	1	13
2.5	--	--
2.75	2	12
3	--	11
3.25	3	10
3.5	4	--
3.75	5	9
4	6	8
4.5	7	7
5	8	6
5.5	9	5
6	10	4
6.5	10.5	3
7	--	2
7.5	--	1
8	11	0
9	13	00
10	15	000

A small pair of straight scissors are essential for cutting the ends of yarn, while stitch markers, row counters and a tape measure are all extremely useful when knitting

Large-eyed sewing needles, crochet hooks and bobbins, which look a little like plastic coloured fish!

Yarns

From the humble budget double knit to the exotic designer furs, there is a vast array of yarns to cover every taste and budget. If you can wrap it around a needle, you can knit it.

Yarns, naturally, are the staple of knitting and choosing the right yarn for the finished item is vital if a specific tension (gauge) is required. Yarns are available in standard weights from a fine 2ply, that allows super shawls and heirloom knitting, to a rope-like thickness in the super chunky, a robust and incredibly quick way of creating a full-length coat. A cushion that is made in an Aran (Fisherman) weight will come out completely differently if knitting in double knit. Yarns can be used in a single strand or a couple of strands together depending on the look of the final piece.

Yarn thickness is classified in different ways on some patterns and it is useful to have an idea of the thickness required. The following table is a rough guide to yarn thickness in the UK and US.

US	UK
Sport	4ply
Knitting worsted	DK (double knit)
Fisherman	Aran
Bulky	Chunky
Super bulky	Super chunky

Yarn content also affects the finished look of the piece. A cotton or silk yarn gives a crisp finish with a defined look to the stitch whereas a woollen yarn is more subtle and diffused. Fashionable furs and textured yarns do lots of the work themselves and simple stitching can be used whilst still creating interesting and textured knitting. Fashion yarns can be found in a range of thicknesses.

Care labels should always be considered when choosing yarn. If the work is going to be constantly cleaned then it may be better to find a yarn that is suitable for a gentle wash cycle. The ball band (yarn label) will give you this information at a glance.

Make the most of small amounts of yarn with different textural effects by mixing them together. A simple way to use odds and ends would be to cast on a few stitches and knit stripes in different yarns of toning colours. Tension in this case would be less important as the different yarns would work differently on the needles. Choose a needle that would complement all of the yarns.

Knitting more than one strand of yarn together can create different effects. In the case of the D-ring bag the yarn has been used double throughout the work in order to create a firm fabric.

Knitting one strand of two different yarns can create a completely different look. Knitting plain and/or fancy yarns at the same time creates a really stunning effect. Scarves knitted in this way make brilliant easy handmade presents.

15

Embellishments

As a self-confessed 'bits and pieces' addict, personalizing work is one of my favourite parts of any craft. Creating an individual piece gives me great satisfaction. A standard cardigan or sweater can be given a whole new look with the right embellishments. A scarf or box can be completely transformed by adding beads, buttons and ribbons. Even a trip to the hardware store can yield interesting items with which to accessorize a piece of knitting.

Beads

Easy to find in almost any size, shape or form, these simple items can lift any work, from a simple mat to a full-length coat. They can be knitted into the work or can be added later. (Both techniques are shown within the projects.)

Braid and ribbon

A trip to a haberdashery will offer plenty of
inspiration. Colourful ribbons in a variety of sizes are
a must in any craft box. Woven or plaited together
they give a more robust finish and can be added to
the project once everything else is finished.

Buttons

A good button stash is a must for any budding
knitting enthusiast. Buttons are not only for
fastening, they are for trimming and embellishing.
Specialist stores and craft fairs are great sources of
handmade buttons but it is also worth trying small
markets and charity shops, as well as asking around
your family to see if any older relations have vintage collections they are willing to share with you.
Vintage buttons are often handmade and will bring a real note of individuality to your chosen piece.

Odds and ends

Furnishing braids, bits of leather and interesting fabrics are another good way to add detail and texture
to a knitted piece. Always check the suitability of the material before adding to a project. There is no
point adding a wonderful finishing touch if you are going to have to remove it before washing.

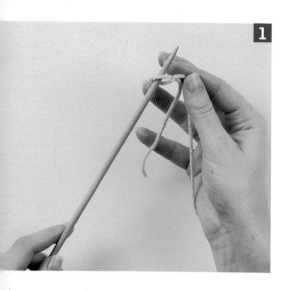

Having selected the yarn and armed ourselves with needles we are ready to create. It would be useful at this stage to say that this book is predominantly written for the right-hander. For left-handed knitting all the instructions should be reversed and it may be useful to look at the step-by-step photographs through a mirror to get a true sense of the way to form stitches and patterns.

CASTING ON

Casting on the number of stitches required for the design is the very first thing we need to do. There are two simple ways of doing this, the cable and thumb methods.

Cable cast-on is done on two needles and works from the end of the yarn.

Make a slip stitch loop and place this onto the left-hand needle, then pull the loop so that it fits around the needle neatly but not tightly; this forms the first stitch **1**. Place the left hand on the needle holding the short yarn along the needle length. Push the right-hand needle between the yarn and the left needle and wrap the ball end of the yarn around the right needle. Pull through to the front to form a second loop and then slip this newly created stitch onto the left needle **2**. Push the right needle front to back between the two stitches now on the left needle and repeat until all the stitches required are on the left needle **3**.

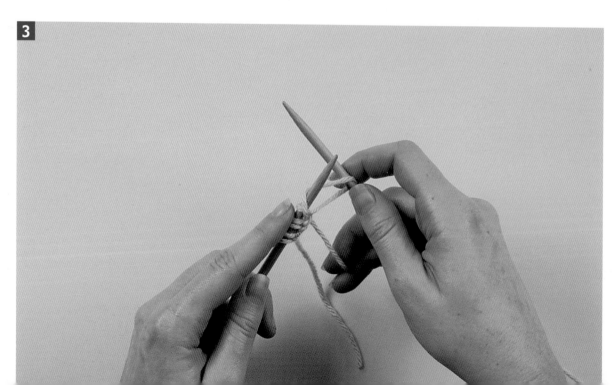

Thumb cast on requires only one needle. Pull off a long length of yarn (enough to cover the amount of stitches – this is a best guess but is approximately two to three times the finished width of the piece. Wrap the shorter end around the thumb of your left hand twice making a cross over 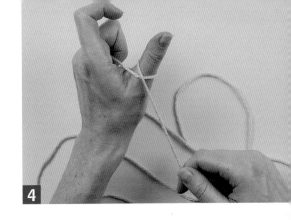. Push the needle against the thumb, over the loose yarn and under the yarn wrapping around the thumb **5**. Using the ball end of the yarn wrap this around the needle under to over and pull through to make a stitch **6**. Pull gently on the shorter yarn to make the stitch sit neatly but not tightly around the needle **7**. Alternatively, make a slip stitch on the needle as the first stitch **8** and then cross the yarn over your thumb and continue as before **9**. Continue in this way until all the stitches required for the piece are on the needle. Do not worry if there is a long length of yarn at the end, this can be used for sewing later.

The method of casting on is a completely personal preference, although the cable cast-on is not as flexible as the thumb.

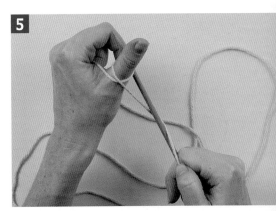

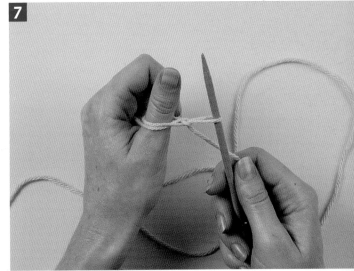

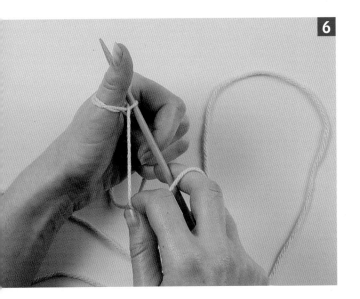

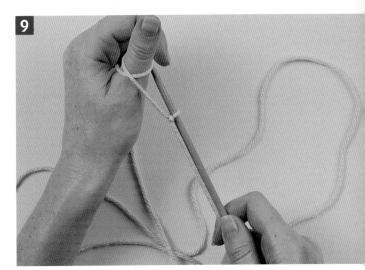

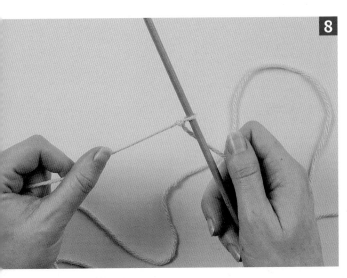

THE KNIT STITCH

The backbone of knitting, the knit stitch, is worked in the same way as the cable cast-on but this time the needle is pushed through the stitches instead of between the stitches.

With the yarn at the back of the work push the needle through from the left to the right of the cast-on stitch on the cast-on row (or stitch from previous row) **1**. Wrap the yarn around the needle under to over and pull through to the front **2 3**. Drop the cast-on stitch from the left needle **4**. Continue along the entire length of the cast-on row.

Working in knit stitch only is called garter stitch.

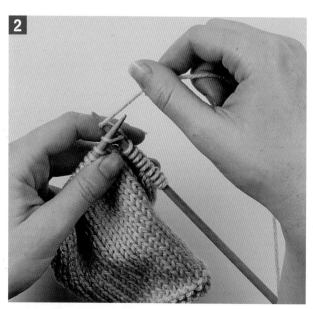

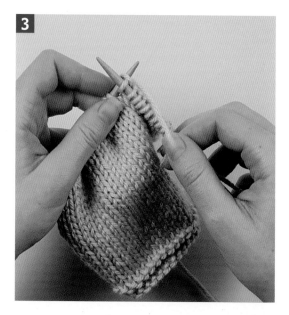

THE PURL STITCH

The purl stitch is the partner to the knit stitch and is worked in reverse. With the yarn to the front of the work push the needle through from the right to the left of the cast-on stitch (or stitch from previous row) **1**. Wrap the yarn around the needle over to under and pull through the stitch **2 3**. Drop the cast-on stitch from the left needle **4**. Continue along the entire length of the cast-on row.

Working one row of knit stitch and one row of purl stitch is known as stocking stitch and is the basis of many patterns.

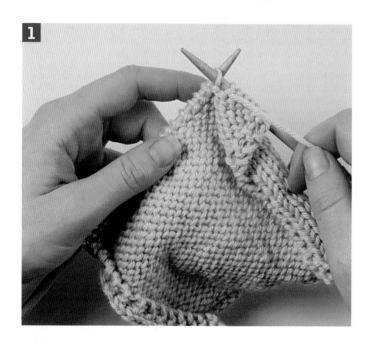

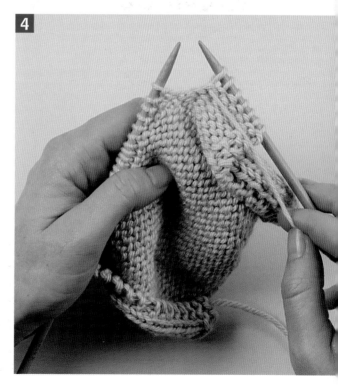

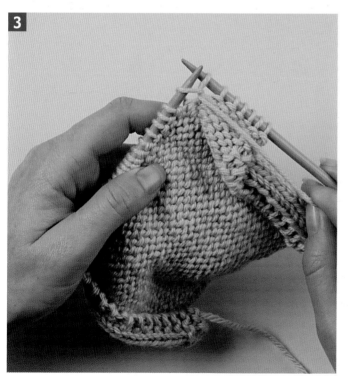

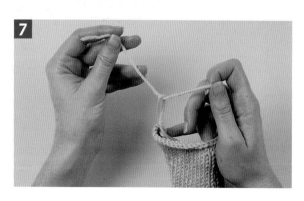

CASTING OFF

Casting off finishes the project piece so that it won't unravel. Cast-off can be worked on either knit or purl rows or in the pattern combination being used to create the project.

Work the first two stitches in the normal way **1**. Lift the first stitch over the second stitch and off the needle **2**. Work the next stitch from the left and repeat the lifting off process **3** **4** **5**. Continue along the row until there is one stitch left on the right-hand needle. Pull up on the needle to elongate this stitch slightly and cut the yarn from the ball, leaving a few inches of yarn **6**. Remove the stitch from the needle and thread the end of the yarn through the loop **7**. Pull up to tighten and knot off the work **8**.

Any ends not used in sewing pieces together can be woven onto the back of the work for a neat and secure finish.

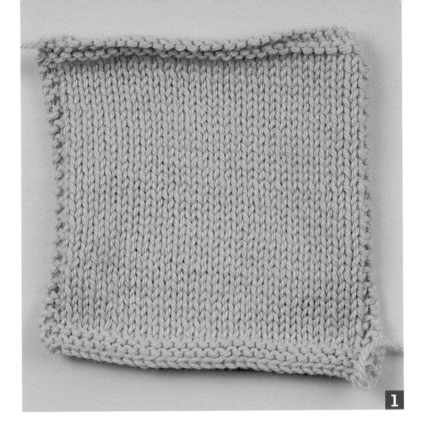

TENSION

A good standard tension gives your work a clean line and holds it in a workable state whilst producing the correct look and feel for the design **1**.

To test tension it is always best to make a tension swatch before beginning on the full project. Usually a swatch is made in the pattern stitch or in a knit a row, purl a row stocking stitch. From this a 4in (10cm) square is marked and the stitches and rows can be counted and compared to the pattern.

If the tension is too loose the finished item will be larger and the fabric will be too floppy and loose **2**. If it is too tight the item will be too firm and smaller than the original pattern **3**.

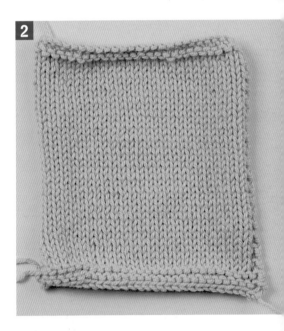

Tension can be easily rectified at the swatch stage by either increasing or decreasing the needle size. If you have a tighter tension than is stated increase the size of the needle and reduce the size of the needle if the tension is looser than required.

There are occasions when a standard tension is not used. This is usually if the original design calls for a very floppy fabric. The tension on scarves, for example, is often purposely loosened to create a softer effect to the final knitted fabric, and similarly, a tight tension might be called for if the piece is to stand up such as with boxes.

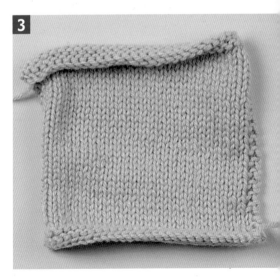

Using more than one strand of yarn at a time can dramatically change tension.

SLIP STITCHES

Both patterns and shaping call for the use of slipped stitches, which can be made on both knit and purl rows. Simply slip the next stitch on the holding needle onto the working needle **1** **2**. When used for shaping the project they are used in conjunction with other stitches and can then be passed over worked stitches and off the needle. In the case of using them for patterns they can work as a backing for beads.

DECREASING

Used as a way of shaping, decreasing can be at the beginning or end of a row or within the row. When a pattern calls for a shape change at the beginning and the end of a row, decreasing takes the form of casting off. Within the row working more than one stitch at a time will create a decrease **1**. It can be used in conjunction with the slip stitch to neatly remove more than one stitch, as in the case of 'sl **2**, k2tog **3**, psso **4**, which allows even removal of two stitches within a row.

INCREASING

The opposite of decreasing this can be worked by casting on at the beginnings and ends of rows for the number of stitches desired or can be worked into rows in various ways. Two ways of doing this are to make one when a loop is pulled from below the row being worked on with the holding needle and a stitch knitted into the back of this loop **1 2**.

An alternative increase is to knit into the front and the back of one stitch before allowing it to drop off the holding needle **3 4 5 6**. This works very well when working in garter stitch.

YARN FORWARD AND YARN BACK

Moving the yarn to the front and the back between the needles is another way of increasing stitches within a row but is more often used in conjunction with other stitches to form patterns, eyelets and buttonholes. On a knit row, bring the yarn to the front of the work between the needles and continue knitting, taking the yarn over the top of the working needle when knitting the next stitch **1** **2**. On the return row work into the back of this stitch. This increases by one stitch. On a purl row, wrapping the yarn around the working needle before continuing onto the next stitch forms the extra stitch **3** **4** **5**.

Eyelets and buttonholes use a combination of moving the yarn to form a stitch whilst decreasing in the next stitches. For example, on a knit row, bring the yarn forward between the needles, knit the next two stitches together. On the next row work the stitch as the pattern suggests. This leaves a small eyelet within the row that can be used as part of the pattern without any further work or used to thread ribbons or braids or to fasten buttons.

CABLES

Used to introduce pattern and rope-like textures to the work, moving stitches onto a separate (cable) needle holds them securely whilst working other stitches around them **1 2**. The stitches on the cable needle are then worked back into the row **3**. Cabling brings the work in tighter and so extra stitches are added into the pattern to keep the size correct. There are many cable patterns making rope, trellis and knot designs into the finished piece **4**.

Using the C4B or C4F instructions can form a simple rope design. C4B works up to the stitches that require the cable. Slip the next two stitches onto the cable needle and leave at the back of the work. Work the next two stitches and then the stitches from the cable needle. C4F is worked in the same way but the cable needle is left at the front of the work.

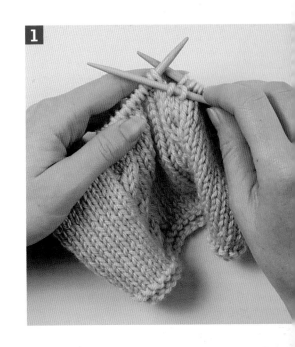

KNITTING BEADS

You will need to plan carefully when knitting beads into a piece of work and decide in advance exactly where you want them to be. In a right-side row knit to where the bead is required then take the yarn to the front (face) of the work and slide a bead so that it sits close to the working needle **1**. Slip the next stitch and return the yarn to the back **2 3**. Continue working the row repeating this process where necessary **4**. On the next row work all the slipped stitches back into the pattern. The slipped stitch sits behind the bead holding it in place.

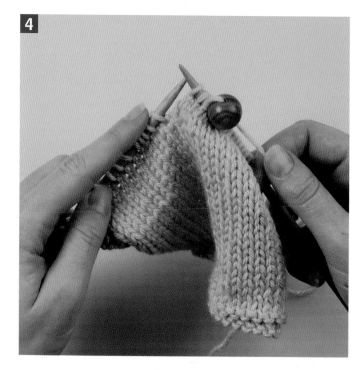

SHORT ROWS

Short rows give shape to the project from the sides allowing greater fit. Work the number of stitches required, bring the yarn between the needles to the front of the work **1**, slip the next stitch **2**, return the yarn between the needles to the back of the work and pass the slipped stitch back to the left (non-working needle) **3**. If working in garter stitch the yarn will need to be passed through the needles again to continue **4** **5** **6**. Wrapping the yarn around a slip stitch in this way eliminates undesirable holes in the finished item.

JOINING PIECES

There are several ways of joining pieces to give a smooth appearance. Mattress (ladder) stitch gives a neat almost invisible seam and is worked on the right side. Lay the pieces to be joined next to each other with the right sides uppermost. Bring the thread up to the right side of one piece. Pick up a stitch from the edge of the adjoining piece and pull through but do not tighten it at this stage **1**. Cross directly back to the first piece and pick up a stitch from the edge **2**. Continue in this way working across the two pieces to form a ladder for a few stitches. Pull up so that the pieces butt against each other **3**. Care must be taken not to pull too tightly or the seam formed will be too tight causing a distortion in the finished piece.

Backstitch is worked with the right sides together and through both the pieces at once **4**. Pin or tack the pieces together. Insert the needle from the back to the front two rows from the end. Push the needle to the back one row from the edge and then up again three rows from the edge **5**. Push back in again at the starting position. Continue in this way for the whole seam pushing the needle from the front to the back where the last stitch was formed and from the back to the front one row away from the last stitch.

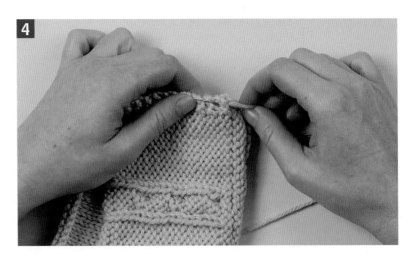

Abbreviations

At first glance the abbreviations in knitting patterns can look a little like some sort of secret code, but you will find that you soon grow used to them. They are, in the main, standard. This table shows commonly used abbreviations.

alt	alternate	s	slip stitch
beg	begin	st st	stocking stitch
cm	centimetres	tbl	through the back of the loop
dec	decrease	tog	together
foll	following	WS	wrong side (or reverse)
inc	increase	yb	yarn back
K	knit	yf	yarn forward
P	purl	yfrn	yarn forward then wrap around working needle
psso	pass slip stitch over		
rem	remaining	C4F	cable 4 forward
RS	right side (or face)	C4B	cable 4 back

Useful Terminology

Not all terminology is the same. Knitting, like anything else, is now an easily accessible craft with books and patterns and yarns available the world over. The internet allows some patterns to be downloaded and the terminology may differ slightly to that of a pattern created in your own country. Yarn can be bought direct from source from manufacturers across the world. The tables below and on page 13 show some of these differences.

US	UK	US	UK
yarn label	ball band	face	right side
bind off (BO)	cast off	reverse	wrong side
shade	colour	stockinette stitch	stocking stitch (st st)
work straight	continue without further shaping	gauge	tension

The terms used for yarn thicknesses (see page 13) are only an approximation and tension squares should be worked before buying sufficient yarn to complete the project. Remember – changing the yarn may change the size.

34

36

38

42

44

46

52

54

58

66

70

72

PROJECTS

PATCHWORK BLANKET

A cosy blanket is not only practical but can add style to a relaxed interior. This simple design uses different sizes of knitted panels, joined in such a way as to provide lots of interest without changing stitches.

Finished size

- Approximately 32 x 24in
  (81 x 86cm)

You will need...

Materials

- Sirdar Snuggly DK – 55% nylon, 45% acrylic, approx 175m per 50g ball
- 2 x 50g balls in each of 388 Vanilla (A), 344 Oatmeal (B), 237 Mole (C) and 379 Stone (D)
- 1 pair 4mm (US6, UK8) needles

Tension

- 22 sts and 45 rows to 4in (10cm) measured over garter stitch using 4mm needles
- Use larger or smaller needles if necessary to obtain the correct tension

Techniques used

- Garter stitich
- Patchwork

Alternative

Use any standard double knit yarn for the blanket. An Aran yarn (using appropriate needle sizes for the weight of yarn) would increase the size and make a fantastic floor rug or wall hanging, for which you could get really creative with colour and tones.

1 For panel 1 cast on 46 sts and work in garter stitch for 90 rows. Cast off.

2 For panel 2 cast on 24 sts and work in garter stitch for 90 rows. Cast off.

3 For panel 3 cast on 46 sts and work in garter stitch for 45 rows. Cast off.

4 Work the following number of panels in different colours:-
A: 4 x panel 1
B: 2 x panel 2, 2 x panel 3
C: 1 x panel 1, 2 x panel 2, 2 x panel 3
D: 2 x panel 1, 2 x panel 3.

Making up

5 Following the diagram (pages 76–77) stitch all panels together using mattress stitch .

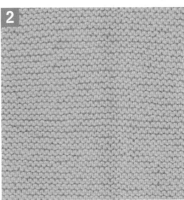

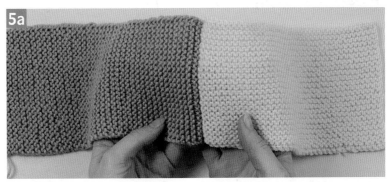

BABY BLOCK

Tension is an important part of knitting as it defines the finished look
and feel of the garment. This baby block is a fun way to practise. Choose
whichever colours you like for this delightful toy.

Finished size

Cube sides approx 4 x 4
[6 x 6]in (10 x 10[15 x 15]cm)

NB Figures in square brackets refer to
larger size, where there is only one set
of figures this applies to all sizes.

You will need...

Materials

- Jaeger Aqua Cotton – 100%
  mercerized cotton (approx
  106m per 50g ball)
- 1 x 50g ball in each of 301
  Crème (A), 317 Blue agate
  (B) and 320 Deep (C)
- 1 pair of 4mm (US6, UK8)
  needles
- Toy stuffing

Tension

- 22 sts and 30 rows to 4in
  (10cm) measured over
  stocking stitch using 4mm
  needles
- Use larger or smaller
  needles if necessary to
  obtain the correct tension

Techniques used

- Stocking stitch
- Layering

Knitting note

- Patterns used: stocking
  stitch (st st). Knit 1 row,
  purl 1 row. Repeat these 2
  rows throughout

Alternative

Make several blocks of
different colours and hang
them to make a baby mobile.

1 Make 2 large panels in
each of A, B and C. Using
A, B or C cast on 24[35] sts
and starting with a knit row,
work in st st for 4[6]in
(10[15]cm). Cast off.

2 Make 2 small panels in
each of A, B and C. Using
A, B or C cast on 13[17] sts
and starting with a knit row,
work in st st for 2[3]in
(5[7.5]cm). Cast off.

Making up

3 Attach the smaller panels
to the larger panels as
diamonds, contrasting the
colours. Join the panels
together to form a cube,
leaving one side of the last
face open for stuffing **3a** **3b**
3c **3d** **3e**.

4 Stuff with toy stuffing and
close the final panel.

3a

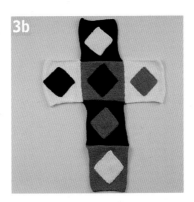
3b

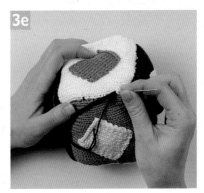
3c

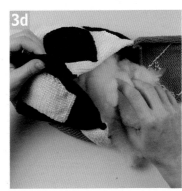
3d

3e

TRINKET BOXES

These boxes can be made to suit any bedroom dressing table, but would look just as good holding pot-pourri in any other room. Using the yarn double gives a firm fabric that will stand up well.

You will need...

Materials

- Craft cotton (used double throughout), two balls
- Cording to complement room colour scheme
- 1 pair of 4.5mm (US7, UK7) needles
- 14mm (US6, UK8) crochet hook
- 19 stitches and 36 rows to 4in (10cm)

Techniques used

- Strengthening yarn by using 2 plys together

Knitting note

The box can be made in three sizes, the measurements for the two larger being shown in brackets

Alternative

Craft cotton is extremely hardwearing and can be obtained in a number of colours, for a softer look with a similar strength other cotton yarns can be used instead.

1 Make two side panels. Using yarn double cast on 11 (16, 21) stitches.

2 Slipping the first stitch of every row, work in garter stitch for 2in (3in, 4in). Cast off **2a 2b**.

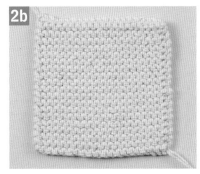

3 Make the bottom and side panels in one. Cast on 11 (16, 21) stitches.

4 Slipping the first stitch in every row work in garter stitch for 6in (9in, 12in). Cast off.

Making up

5 Using mattress stitch join the long panel around three sides of each of the smaller side panels forming a box.

6 Cut the cording to the required length and stitch or bind the ends to avoid fraying. Stitch to the top edges of the boxes.

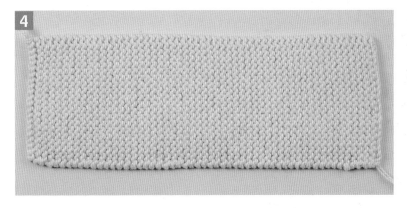

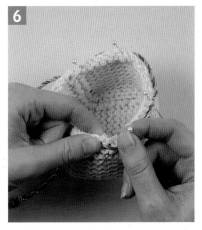

SLIP STITCH SCARF

The use of a simple slip stitch pattern gives texture to this otherwise plain scarf. The look is complex but the make is simplicity itself. The yarn is chunky and the fringing is heavy for a real winter warmer.

Finished size

Without fringing approx
6½ x 33in (16.5 x 84cm)

You will need...

Materials

- Rowan chunky print, 100% wool approx 109yd (100m) per 100g ball
- 2 x 100g balls in 078 Pebble dash
- 1 pair 9mm (US13, UK00) needles

Tension

- 11 sts and 14 rows to 4in (10cm) measured over slip stitch patt

Techniques used

- Manipulating yarn to create patterns

Tip

For a more defined slip stitch pattern use a flatter yarn. Sirdar Denim Ultra works easily as well, but remember when changing the yarn and needles the size of the finished piece will alter.

1 Cast on 18 sts and knit one row, then purl one row.

2 1st row: K4 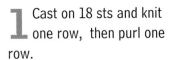 *yf 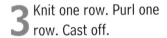, slip 2 [2c], yb; rep from * to last 4 sts, K4
2nd row: K1, purl to last st, K1
3rd row: K2, yf, slip 2, yb; rep to last 2 sts, K2
4th row: As 2nd row
These 4 rows form patt and are rep throughout.
Continue in pattern until scarf measures approx 33in (84cm) ending with the second row of patt.

3 Knit one row. Purl one row. Cast off.

4 With the remainder of the yarn cut a fringe 8½in (21cm) long.

5 Heavily fringe around the two short ends and one long edge of the scarf [5a] [5b].

2a

2b

2c

5a

5b

SHORT ROW HAT

Short rows create the shaping in this hat, which is knitted from side to side. Silk Garden gives a stripe effect while Blossom adds lots of rich texture to this simple design.

You will need...

Materials
- Noro Silk Garden –
  45% silk, 45% kid mohair,
  10% lambswool approx
  110yd (100m) per 50g ball
  or Noro Blossom –
  40% wool, 30% kid mohair,
  20% silk,
  10% nylon approx 98yd
  (90m) per 50g ball
- 2 x 50g balls
- 1 pair 4.5mm (US7, UK7)
  needles

Tension
- 18 stitches and 34 rows to
  4in (10cm) measured over
  garter stitch using 4.5mm
  needles

Techniques used
- Short rows

Knitting note
- Stitch used: garter stitch
  (knit each row)

Tip

The yarns can be
interchanged without any
difference to the size of the
finished hat.

1 Cast on 31 sts.

2 Work in pattern:
1st and 2nd row: Knit
3rd row: K22 turn
4th row: K22
5th row: K27 turn
6th row: K27
7th row: K22 turn
8th row: K22
9th–12th Rows: Knit.

3 Continue in patt until the longer edge of the hat measures 22in (56cm) ending with the last row of the pattern. Cast off.

4 Run a length of yarn through the short edge top of the hat 4a, pull up and fasten off 4b.

Making up

5 Join the cast-on and cast-off edges.

BUTTONHOLE CUSHION

Buttons combined with rich ribbon and braid make this cushion a joy. The stitch is kept simple to enhance the embellishment. Worked in a single piece, this is a quick project with minimal making up.

Finished size

Approx 16in (41cm) square

You will need...

Materials

- Rowan Chunky print, 100% wool approx 109yd (100m) per 100g ball
- 4 x 100g balls in 078 Pebble dash
- 1 pair 9mm (US13, UK00) needles
- Approx 1yd (1m) 1½in (4cm) wide decorative braid and/or ribbon for threading
- 8 buttons to match
- 1 x 16in (41cm) cushion pad
- 1 x zip to fit

Tension

- 11 sts and 14 rows to 4in (10cm) measured over st st using 9mm needles

Technique used

- Making buttonholes

Knitting note

- When knitting across the 3 cast-on stitches knit into the back of the stitch **1d**

Tip

Inserting the cushion pad before threading the braid and/or ribbon ensures that the cushion is held under the correct tension and will not be pulled out of shape or the braids threaded too tightly.

1 Cast on 43 sts and work 4 rows of st st
5th and 9th rows: K21, cast off 3 sts **1a** **1b**, K21
6th and 10th rows: P21, cast on 3 sts **1c**, P21
7th and 8th rows: st st
Work in patt for 32in (81cm) ending with the first 4 rows of st st.

2 Cast off.

Making up

3 Stitch the zip into place along the cast-on and cast-off (bind-off) edges of the cushion cover. Open the zip.

4 With RS together sew the sides of the cushion into place. Turn through.

5 Insert the cushion pad and close the zip.

6 Thread the ribbon or braid through the buttonholes and neaten the edges **6a**. Hold in place with buttons or small stitches **6b**.

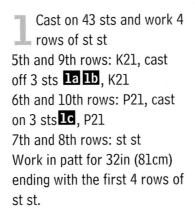

1a

1b

1c

1d

6a

6b

45

FLUFFY CUSHION

A soft and cuddly cushion to snuggle up with on a cold winter evening.
This piece has the feel of a warming hot water bottle and looks stylish
as well as cosy, thanks to the intarsia work on the corner.

Finished size

Approx 13 x 13in (33 x 33cm)

You will need...

Materials

- Wendy Shimmer 100% Polyester approx 65m per 50g ball
- 3 x 50g balls in Purple Haze (A)
- Wendy Velvet touch 100% Nylon Micro Fibre approx 114 yd (105m) per 50g ball
- 1 x 50g ball in Lilac Velvet (B)
- 1 pair 4.5mm (US7, UK7) needles
- Toy stuffing

Tension

- 19 sts and 29 rows to 4in (10cm) measured over st st using 4.5mm needles

Technique used

- Intarsia

Knitting note

- Stitch used: st st

Alternative

Make cushion squares in single colours and textures or change the yarns over to make a set of similar toning cushions.

1 Using A cast on 57 sts and knit 1 row then purl 1 row.

2 Next row: K56 A, join B, K1 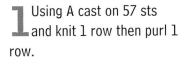.
Next row: P1 B, P56 A.
Next row: K56 A, K1 B.
Next row: P2 B, P55 A.
Next row: K55 A, K2 B.
Next row: P2 B, P55 A.
Next row: K54 A, K3 B.
Next row: P3 B, K54 A.
Next row: K54 A, P3 B.

3 Keeping continuity of pattern correct, inc the number of sts using B on next and every 3rd row, until there are 28 stitches in A and 29 stitches in B **3a** **3b**.

4 Work 1 row and cast off.

5 Repeat steps 1–5 to make the second side.

Making up

6 Sew three sides of the cushion together, loosely stuff with the toy stuffing **6a** and close the fourth side **6b**.

PATCHWORK BAG

Intarsia work means this funky bag can be made without the need for lots of seaming. Wooden handles complete the look.

Finished size

Max width 9in (23cm) x 8in (20.5cm) deep (excl handles)

You will need...

Materials

- Sirdar Tuscany 57% polyester, 38% acrylic, 5% nylon approx 57m per 50g ball
- 1 x 50g ball in each of 664 Baccarat (A), 665 Gypsy (B)
- 2 x 50g ball in 661 Jasper (C)
- 1 pair 8mm (US11, UK0)
- Wooden handles approx 4 x 5½in (10 x 14cm)
- Piece of plastic canvas approx 8 x 2¾in (20.5 x 7cm) to form base
- Lining fabric approx 20 x 18in (51 x 46cm)

Technique used

- Intarsia

Knitting note

- Stitch used: st st

Alternative

Working the bag in a single colour would allow coordination with a particular outfit or theme.

Front and back panel

1 Cast on 13 sts B 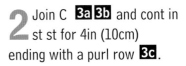 **1a** and 13 sts A **1b**.

2 Work in st st for 3in (7.5cm) ending on a purl row.

2 Join C **3a** **3b** and cont in st st for 4in (10cm) ending with a purl row **3c**.

4 Join B and knit 13 and knit one row of sts, join A and knit to end.

5 Cont in st st for a further 3in (7.5cm) ending with a purl row.

6 Join C and knit to end of row.

7 Next row: P1, P2tog to last st, P1 (14 sts).

8 Cont in st st for 6 rows.

9 Cast off.

Side and bottom panel

10 Cast on 7 sts in C and work in st st for 23in (58cm) ending with a purl row.

11 Cast off.

Making up

12 With right sides together sew the side and lower panel to the front and back panels, making sure the top edges fit smoothly.

13 Cut a piece of plastic canvas 2¹/₂ x 7¹/₂in (6.25 x 19cm) and slip stitch to the inside of bag base.

14 Cut a piece of lining fabric 21 x 18in (53.5 x 46cm). Fold in half lengthways and stitch the side seams, making a pocket **14a**. Stitch diagonally across the corners to form the base of the lining **14b**.

15 Attach the handles firmly to the upper sections of the bag **15a**. Insert lining and slip stitch into place pleating the fabric across the bottom of the handles **15b**.

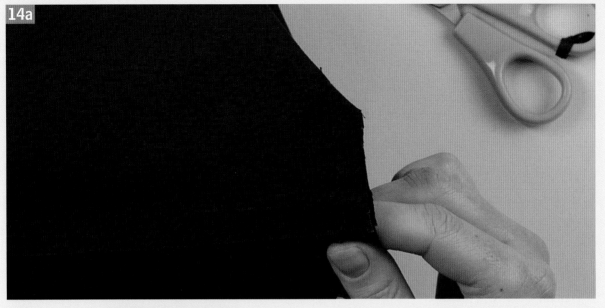

14a

14b

15a

15b

COSY COLLAR

A dramatic collar will set off any item. This one is quick and easy
to create. The addition of beading or a brooch enhances this
fur yarn further.

Finished size

Approx 4 x 23in
(10 x 58cm) before fastening
(easily adjustable)

You will need...

Materials

- Adriafil Fizzy 56% polyammide 28% viscose 16% polyester approx 29¹/₂yd (27m) per 25g ball
- 3 x 25g balls in 80 pink/blue
- 1 pair 9mm (US13, UK00) needles
- 9 buttons to fasten
- 1 fancy brooch or bead embellishment

Techniques used

- Fastening placement
- Embellishing

Knitting note

- Stitch used: garter stitch

Alternative

Make a bold statement with a fun pair of coordinating cuffs (**see right**). Cast on 10 sts. Work in garter stitch for 8in (20.5cm). Cast off. Attach buttons to the underside of the cast-off edge and fasten directly into the stitching on the cast-on edge.

1 Cast on 15 sts.

2 Work in garter stitch for 23in (58cm). Cast off.

Making up

3 Position the corners of each end of the scarf into a point. Mark button points on the reverse side of the upper end **3a**. Stitch buttons into place **3b**.

4 Using the spaces in the knitting fasten buttons.

5 Trim with brooch or beads of choice.

EMBELLISHED BAG

A classic bag is given the designer treatment with the use
of texture and embellishments. Fully lined and of a good size, this bag
makes a statement as well as being practical!

Finished size

Approx 12 x 12in
(30 x 30cm)

You will need...

Materials

- Adriafil Graphic 75% wool, 15% acrylic, 10% polyamide approx 76yd (70m) per 50g ball.
- 3 x 50g balls in 087 Multicolour Fuchsia/Red
- Toning 4ply or double knit yarn for the cord
- 1 pair 5.5mm (US8, UK5) needles
- Buttons and beads to match
- Approx 26 x 26in (63 x 63cm) toning fabric for lining

Tension

- 15 sts x 27 rows to 10cm using 5.5mm needles in garter stitch

Technique used

- Sewn on embellishment

Knitting note

Stitch used: garter stitch

Alternative

Allow your imagination to run wild with extras. Why not use half opened zips or funky ribbons tied in bows to decorate instead of or as well as beads?

Front and back

Work 2 pieces alike.

1 Cast on 42 sts.

2 Work in garter stitch for 10½in (27cm).

3 Next row: K4 **3a**, * K2tog, yfwd **3b**, K2 **3c**, rep from * to last 4 sts, K4.

4 Next row: Knit.

5 Cont in garter stitch until work measures 12in (31cm). Cast off.

3a

3b

3c

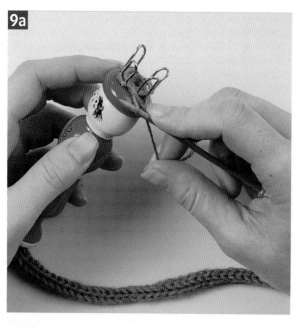

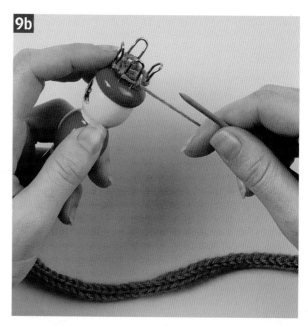

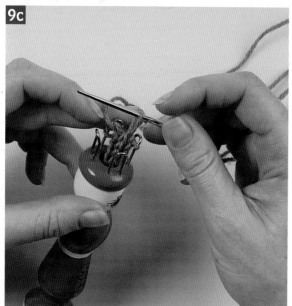

Handle

6 Cast on 7 sts.

7 Work in garter stitch until all the yarn is used leaving enough to cast off.

8 Cast off.

Cord fastening

9 Using a toning yarn work 21in (53.5cm) of dolly bobbin (French knitting) **9a** **9b** and fasten off **9c** **9d**.

Making up

10 Using finished bag pieces as a template cut the fabric to make a lining. Join the seams of the bag and lining.

11 Thread the cord through eyelet holes **11a** **11b**. Finish the cord ends with beads.

12 Randomly embellish the bag with buttons and beads of your choice.

13 Insert lining **13a** and stitch in place then attach handle **13b**.

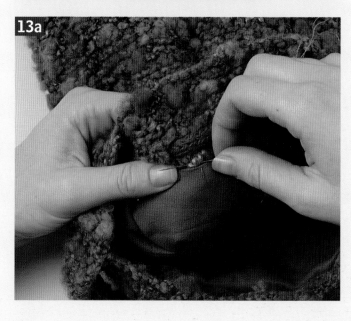

D-RING BAG

With yarn knitted double throughout and with knitted in embellishments, this bag is both hardwearing and elegant. The silver D-rings give it a surprisingly modern twist.

Finished size

Approx 11 x 7^1/$_2$in
(28 x 19cm)

You will need...

Materials

- Sirdar Wash & Wear Double Crepe 55% acrylic, 45% nylon approx 270m per 100g ball
- 2 x 100g balls in 275 black (A)
- Sirdar Boa 100% polyester 93m per 50g ball (Plume or Shimmer could be used instead)
- 1 x 50g ball in 0011 jet black (B)
- 1 pair 4.5mm (US7, UK7) needles
- 14 x 1in (2.5cm) D-rings
- 12in (30cm) of 1^1/$_3$in (3.5cm) wide matching ribbon

Tension

- 19 sts and 36 rows to 4in (10cm) measured over garter stitch

Technique used

- Knitted in embellishments

Knitting note

Stitch used: garter stitch

Alternative

The two yarns used together idea can be the same as the example shown but the use of two yarns of differing colours and/or textures can create surprising results.

Bag

1 Using yarn double cast on 47 sts and work 16 rows in garter stitch.

2 Next row: K21 and insert D-ring over next 5 sts, K21 **2a** **2b** **2c**.

3 Next row: Knit.

4 Next row: K21, insert D-ring over next 5 sts, K21.

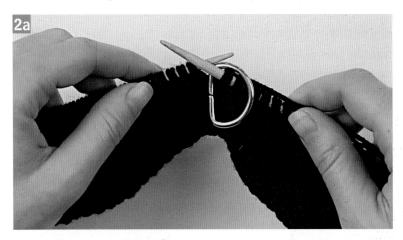

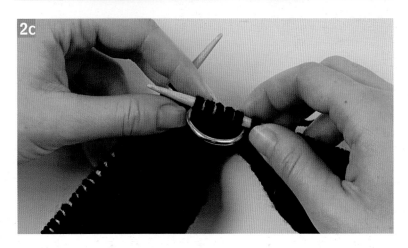

5 Cont in garter stitch for 4¼in (11cm) ending on WS.

6 Change to B and work 3 rows of garter stitch.

7 Change back to A and work one row.

8 Next row: K7, *insert D-ring over next 5 sts, K2; rep from * to last 7 sts, K7.

9 Cont in garter stitch until work measures 6½in (16.5cm).

10 Cast off 4 sts at the beginning of the next 2 rows.

11 Work 12 rows.

12 Cast on 4 sts at the beginning of the next 2 rows.

13 Work 14 rows.

14 Next row: K7, *insert D-ring over next 5 sts, K2; repeat from * to last 7 sts, K7.

15 Knit 1 row.

16 Change to B and complete 3 rows.

17 Change to A and cont in garter stitch until top and bottom of the work measure the same, ending with a WS row.

18 Next row: Cast off 21 sts, knit 5 sts, cast off 21 sts.

19 Fasten off and break yarn.

20 Rejoin yarn to rem 5 sts.

21 Work until strap measures 5in (12.5 cm).

22 Cast off.

60

20

24

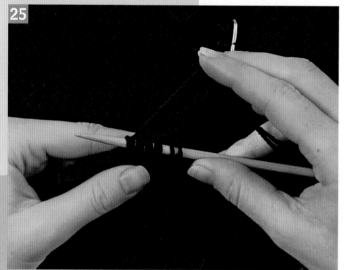
25

30

Making up

23 Using the open bag as a template and omitting the fastening strap cut lining fabric.

24 Join the side seams of the bag together and stitch across the bottom edges.

Handle

25 With right side facing pick up and knit 6 sts across the top of the side seam. Knit for 6in (15cm) then cast off.

26 Rep across the top of the second side seam.

27 Loop the cast-off edges through a D-ring and stitch into place.

28 Cast on 6 sts and knit for 12in (30cm).

29 Cast off.

30 Attach the ends of the strap to the D-rings.

31 Slip stitch the ribbon along the underside of the handle to strengthen.

ZIPPED CUSHION

The use of subtle cable work takes this soft cushion from the ordinary into a stylish addition to the home. Knit up several in a selection of complementary tones to add warmth and style to a living area.

Finished size
Approx 16 x 16in (41 x 41cm)

You will need...

Materials
- Rowan Soft Tweed, 56% wool, 20% viscose, 14% polyamide, 10% silk approx 87yd (80m) per 50g ball
- 3 x 50g balls in 00003 Thistle
- 1 pair 8mm (US11, UK0) needles
- Cable needle for chunky work
- Stitch holders
- 14in (35cm) zip in toning colour
- 1 x 16in (40.5cm) cushion pad

Tension
- 12 sts and 15 rows to 4in (10cm)

Technique used
- Cable

Knitting note
Stitch used: st st

Alternative

This soft cushion can be further enhanced with the attachment of tassels at the corners or toning buttons used in rows to echo the cabling.

Back

1 Cast on 46 sts.

2 Work 6 rows of st st.

3 Cont in pattern:

Next row: K15, C4F **3a 3b**, K3, P2, K3, C4B **3c 3d**, K15
Next row: purl
Next row: K22, P2, K22
Next row: purl
Next row: K22, P2, K22
Next row: purl.

4 Rep patt 8 more times.

5 Work first row of patt once more.

6 Beginning with a purl row cont in st st for 6 rows.

7 Cast off.

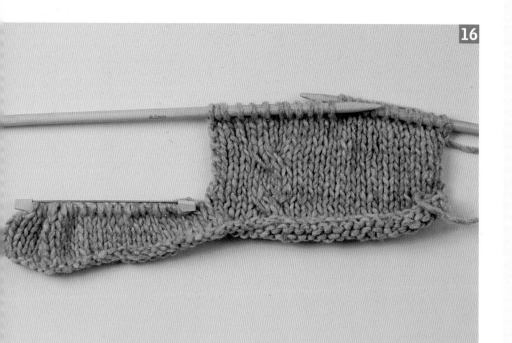

16

Making up

22 Place zip in opening and stitch neatly into place, open the zip.

23 With RS together sew around all four sides of the cushion cover.

24 Turn through, insert cushion pad and close the zip.

Front

8 Cast on 47 sts.

9 Work 6 rows of st st.

10 Next row: K15, C4F, K3, P1, cast off next st p1, K3, C4B, K15.

11 Next row: P23, turn. Place rem sts on a stitch holder.

12 Next row: P1, K22.

13 Next row: Purl.

14 Next row: P1, K22.

15 Next row: Purl.

16 Rep patt 8 more times.

17 Break yarn and leave these sts on a stitch holder.

18 Rejoin yarn to rem 23 sts and purl to end.

19 Cont in patt to match and mirror the first side.

20 Next row: K15, C4F, K3, P1 cast on 1 st then from the stitch holder, P1, K3, C4B, K15 (47 sts).

21 Beg with a purl row work 6 rows of st st and cast off.

CABLE BAG

Raffia is a fantastic material to use for summer items. Contrasting it with
a fluffy yarn gives this fun bag a delightful mix of textures and the
coordinated gingham lining completes the look.

Finished measurement

Approx 10½ x 7½in
(27 x 19cm)

You will need...

Materials

- Adriafil Rafia, 100% wood pulp
- 2 x 25g skeins in Black (A)
- Adriafil Fizzy, 56% polyammide 28% viscose 16% polyester approx 29½yd (27m) per 50g ball
- 1 x 50g ball in black
- 1 pair of 5mm (US8, UK6) needles
- 9¾in (25cm) lining fabric to match
- 2 x 8¾in (5 x 22cm) piece of plastic canvas

Technique used

- Cable

Tension

- 16 sts and 20 rows to 4in (10cm) measured over st st

Knitting note

Pattern used: st st
Preparation: wind the rafia into balls

Back

1 Using A, cast on 34 sts.

2 Work in st st for 6in (15cm).

3 Change to Fizzy and work a further 1¼in (4cm).

4 Cast off.

Front

5 Cast on 36 sts.

6 Cont in the cable patt:
1st row: Knit
2nd row: Purl
3rd row: K13, P1, C8F **6a 6b**, P1, K13
4th row: Purl.

7 Work in cable patt 8 times then 1st 2 rows of patt again.

8 Change to B and work a further 1¼in (4cm).

9 Cast off.

Handle and sides

10 Using A, cast on 7 sts.

11 Work in st st for 39in (100cm).

12 Cast off.

Making up

13 Cut a piece of lining that is 7 x 9¾in (18 x 25cm). Completely cover the plastic canvas with fabric and sew securely into place.

14 Sew the handle to the sides of the front and back pieces.

15 With right sides together sew the bag to the base section.

18

16 Cut a piece of lining 7 x 24in (18 x 61cm). Sew the short ends together to form a tube.

17 Pin and tack to the base section of the bag covering all showing seams and slip stitch into place 17.

18 Turn a seam at the loose edge and slip stitch to the top of the raffia.

19 Pull the handle slightly to cause it to curve along the length.

CABLE HAT

This cloche-style hat employs cable stitches and textural interest to bring out the versatility of an Aran-weight yarn in a style that suits everyone.

Finished size

Diameter at widest point
11½in (29cm)
Depth 8in (20.5cm)

You will need...

Materials

- Rowan All Seasons Cotton, 60% cotton, 40% acrylic approx 98yd (90m) per 50g ball
- 1 x 50g ball in 211 Blackcurrant
- 1 pair each of 4mm (US6, UK8) and 5mm (US8, UK6) needles

Tension

- 18 sts and 24 rows to 4in (10cm) over st st using 4mm needles

Technique used

- Cable

Knitting note

- Stitch: moss stitch

Alternative

An extra vintage flourish can be added to this classic hat by the use of knitted, crochet or false flowers attached to one side only.

1 Using 4mm needles cast on 97 sts.

2 Work in moss stitch for 1¼in (4cm). Each row: K1 (P1, K1) to end.

3 Next row: Work 11 sts, m1, (work 15 sts, m1) 5 times, work 11 sts (103 sts).

4 Work in cable pattern:
1st row: Knit
2nd row: K9, P8 to last st, K1
3rd row: Rep 1st row
4th row: Rep 2nd row
5th row: K1, (C8B **4a**, K9 **4b**) 6 times
6th row: As 2nd row
7th row: As 1st row
8th row: As 2nd row
Cont in patt until work measures 6in (15cm) ending with 8th row of pattern.

5 To shape the top of the hat – next row: K1, *K2, (k2tog) twice, K4, k2tog, K1, K2tog, K2, rep from * to end (79 sts).

6 Next row: (K7, p6) 6 times, K1.

7 Next row: K1, *K1, (K2 tog) twice, K1, (K1, K2tog) twice, K1, rep from * to end (55 sts).

8 Next row: (K5, p4) 6 times, K1.

9 Next row: K1, *(K2tog) twice, K2tog, K1, K2tog, rep from * to end (31 sts).

10 Next row: (K3, P2,) 6 times, K1.

11 Next row: K1, *K2 tog, K3 tog, rep from * to end (13 sts).

12 Break yarn and run through sts, pull up and tie off **12a**. Sew back seam **12b**.

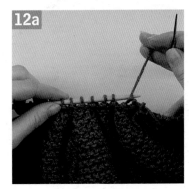

FUN FUR SCARF

This light and airy scarf is made using just one ball of yarn. The glamourous light-reflective yarn makes it a fun accessory that looks just as good at a party as on a cold day!

Finished size
Approx 5 x 55in (13 x 140cm)

You will need...

Materials
- Wendy Chic, 60% nylon, 30% polyester, 10% metalised polyester, approx 80m per 50g ball
- 1 x 50g ball in Monet
- 1 pair 10mm (US15, UK000) needles

Technique used
- Wrap and drop

Tip

It is important to hold onto the stitches whilst working this loose pattern. Care must be taken at all times to ensure that extra loops are not dropped on the 4th row.

Alternative

This versatile stitch pattern can be used to make scarves and light as a feather shawls but increasing the number of stitches will mean more balls of yarn are required. For a shawl double the number of stitches and work in the same way. You will need 4 balls.

1 Cast on 15 sts.

2 1st row: Knit
2nd row: Knit.

3 3rd row: *K1, yfrn 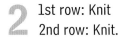 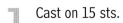; rep from * to last stitch, K 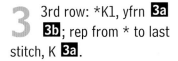.

4 4th row: *K1, drop the wrapped sts from the left needle **4a**; rep from * to last st, K1 **4b**.

5 Rep the pattern finishing on a 2nd row until the whole ball has been used.

6 Cast off. (Remember to leave enough yarn to cast off.)

EYELET SCARF

This scarf, or tippett, makes use of a variety of embellishments including ribbons and beads. The preparation is well worth the effort. The yarn is used double throughout to give a full and luxurious finish.

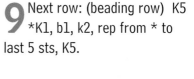

Finished size

Approx 7 x 44in (18 x 112cm)

You will need...

Materials

- Rowan Kidsilk Haze, 70% super kid mohair, 30% silk, approx 229yd (210m) per 25g ball
- 2 x 25g balls in 589 Majestic
- 1 pair 5mm (US8, UK6) needles
- 3yd (3m) of ribbon for threading
- 109 knitting beads

Tension

- 18 sts and 23 rows to 4in (10cm) over st st using 5mm needles

Technique used

- Knitting in beads
- Eyelets

Knitting note

- Stitch used: st st with garter stitch edge

Tip

To position bead. Bring the bead up to the stitches and yarn to the front of the work. Slip the next stitch and take the yarn to the back of the work. This is shown as b1.

1 With the yarn doubled and a fine needle, thread on the beads.

2 Cast on 224 sts and work 4 rows of garter stitch.

3 Next row: (eyelet row) K2, *K1, yf, K2tog, rep from * to last 3 sts, K3.

4 Next row: K2, P to last 2 sts, knit 2.

5 Work next 2 rows in st st with garter stitch edges.

6 Next row: (beading row) K2, *K1, b1 **6a**, K2 **6b**, rep from * to last 3 sts, K3.

7 Next row: K2, P to last 2 sts, K2.

8 Work next 2 rows in st st with garter stitch edging.

9 Next row: (beading row) K5 *K1, b1, k2, rep from * to last 5 sts, K5.

10 Next row: K2, P to last 2 sts, P2.

11 Cont in st st with garter edging until the work measures 6in (15cm).

12 Work an eyelet row as before.

13 Work 4 rows of garter stitch. Cast off.

14 Cut a length of ribbon 45in (114cm) long and thread through the eyelets at the bottom of the scarf/tippet. Secure on the reverse side by stitching.

15 Using the remainder of the ribbon, thread through the top edge of the scarf/tippet leaving the edges free to pull to size and fasten in a bow.

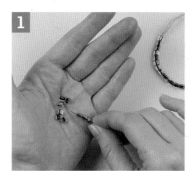

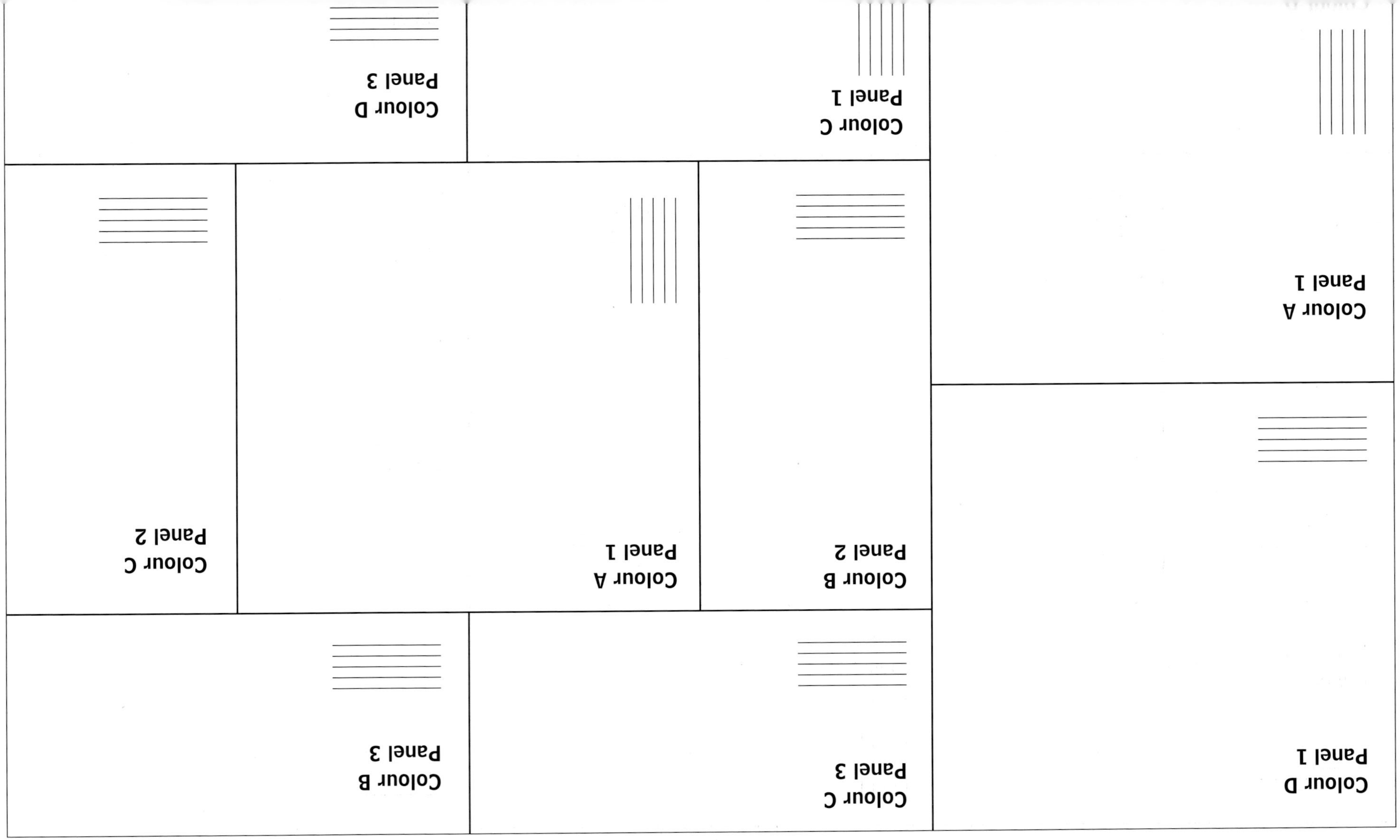

Colour D
Panel 3
Colour C
Panel 1
Colour A
Panel 1
Colour C
Panel 2
Colour A
Panel 1
Colour B
Panel 2
Colour B
Panel 3
Colour C
Panel 3
Colour D
Panel 1

Patchwork Blanket template (see page 34)

Colour A
Panel 1

Colour D
Panel 1

Colour B
Panel 2

Colour C
Panel 3

Colour A
Panel 1

Colour B
Panel 3

Colour C
Panel 2

Colour D
Panel 3

SUPPLIERS

Adriafil
Unit 4
Townhead Trading Centre
Main Street
Addingham
West Yorkshire
LS29 9BZ
01943 432044

Jaeger Yarns
Green Lane Mill
Holmfirth
West Yorkshire
HD9 2DX
01484 680050
01484 680056

Noro Designer Yarns
Units 8–10 Newbridge Industrial Estate
Pitt Street
Keighley
West Yorkshire
BD21 4PQ
01535 644222
lauren@designeryarns.uk.com
www.designeryarns.uk.com

Rowan Yarns
Green Lane Mill
Holmfirth
West Yorkshire
HD9 2DX
01484 681881
mail@knitrowan.co.uk
www.knitrowan.co.uk

Sirdar Spinning Ltd
Flanshaw Lane
Wakefield
West Yorkshire
WFN 9ND
01924 371501
enquiries@sirdar.co.uk
www.sirdar.co.uk

Wendy Wools
Thomas Ramsden & Co Ltd
Netherfield Road
Guiseley
West Yorkshire
LS20 9PD
01943 872264
sales@tbramsden.co.uk
www.tbramsden.co.uk

ACKNOWLEDGEMENTS

Rowan Yarns for their generous sponsorship.
Lesley and Barbara for their help in knitting.
David Bluff at Sew In of Marple for his help, advice and support.
Gerrie Purcell at GMC Publications for her initial commissioning of this book.
Clare Miller at GMC Publications, editor and hand-model, for her patience and expertise.
Anthony Bailey for his wonderful photography.
John Hawkins for his creativity and design of the final book.
And finally, Jon Ransom for his love, care and hand-holding.

GLOSSARY

Cable
Manipulating and crossing stitches into a pattern by use of a cable needle (see equipment).

Cast (bind) off
Finishing a section of knitting.

Cast on
Beginning a section of knitting.

Dropping
Removing the extra loops created during wrapping (see below) when elongating stitches.

Eyelet
Creating buttonholes and/or lacey patterns by the use of moving the yarn forward and knitting more than one stitch together.

Garter stitch
Working every row with a knit stitch. The front (face) and back (reverse) of the work is the same.

Intarsia
Creating blocks of colour and/or texture by combining yarns in the same row.

Knitting in
Placing beads and other embellishments during the knitting process.

Moss stitch
Working alternate knit and purl stitches on the first row and reversing the stitches on the next row. Gives a textured finish.

Short rows
Developing shape by use of part rows.

Slip stitch
Moving one or more stitches from the holding to the working needle without creating a knit or purl stitch.

Stocking stitch
Working one row knit and one row purl. The front (face) of the work is smooth and the back (reverse) is textured.

Wrapping
Creating elongated stitches by wrapping the yarn around the working needle one or more times between worked stitches.

INDEX

For a complete catalogue or to place an order, contact:
GMC Publications, Castle Place, 166 High Street,
Lewes, East Sussex BN7 1XU United Kingdom
Tel: 01273 488005 Fax: 01273 402866
Website: www.gmcbooks.com
Orders by credit card are accepted